# SEX POSITIONS

ILLUSTRATED WITH PICTURES NO NUDITY

Amber Moon

# TABLE OF CONTENTS

# INTRODUCTION

Kama Sutra, it's a naughty but exciting concept that we've nearly all come across but something we also know very little about. Nearly 2000 years ago the elders of various Indian communities began writing a manual that brought together decades of shared wisdom on what they considered to be the most fundamental aspect of a good society: how to have toe-curling great sex. For many of us the Kama Sutra is a series of sometimes terrifying and sometimes appealing sexual positions, usually portrayed by images of stone-faced ancient Indians in various acts of contortion that result in genitals touching. We like to think that if we could master these then we'd hit the secret orgasm button those elders were trying to tell us about. We tend to hate manuals and tests but the exam on exotic sex positions? I'll take that any day.

The original manual is much more than just a sex manual, it is a text that sees good sex as the foundational element of any strong relationship and puts it on almost a magical plain. The Kama Sutra sees sex as a form of communication between lovers that can say truths we hide with words from our mouths. It wants us to see sex as a way of gaining pleasure through the pleasure of another and to learn how to truly be present with our lover. For the Kama Sutra, sex is very much a spiritual act and the true joy of it comes from elevating the physical act of lovemaking to the spiritual one. Many groups have co-opted Kama Sutra but not always with the best intentions. The sex industry and publications like Cosmopolitan like to publish guides and educational videos that titillate their audience, but will always be unsuccessful in teaching the Kama Sutra because they are all about naughtiness and an almost selfish quest for pleasure – not truly connecting with your partner.

While these newer takes on the Kama Sutra miss out on key elements and focus too much on kinkiness, and not actually great sex. There is also a need to update what the original text tells us. It is, frankly, outdated – we've learned a lot about the human anatomy since those early days and a lot of the original text is sexist and, ironically, conservative. It's also possibly a bit unrealistic. We no longer believe that men know everything about sex and they are merely teaching women how to enjoy their bodies – the delicacy and subtlety that is traditionally ascribed to female sexuality has just as much to teach men. Many of us also no longer see quite the same value in marriage or even have the same approach to love as ancient Indians did. A sparingly mentioned fact about ancient Indian culture is that sexual relationships and love were not how we see them, it was rare to meet someone you liked, click, fall in love and then marry. Instead you married and then love was something built together and the Kama Sutra acted as a guide to learning how to discover your partner and to build a connection around your lovemaking.

 All of this means that there is room for a modern approach to the Kama Sutra that utilizes our knowledge of what pleasures are hidden in our body, that tries to use the fruits of both the female and male form to find new ideas for the bedroom, and understands that relationships in the 21<sup>st</sup> century aren't always arranged marriages, but, at the same time, this modern approach is also sensitive to the original desire to create a strong and loving relationship that tries to take lovemaking to the spiritual dimension.

This book will try to maintain this balance and approach to give you a streamlined understanding of the Kama Sutra so you can enjoy its many wonders and also provide lots of fun and sensual positions for you to try out with a partner so that you may better explore and understand each other. The book will begin with a discussion of what Kama Sutra is so you can put its theory into practice, and will also have a section on how to actually get ready to carry out the Kama Sutra. It will then include 40 tantalizing positions that you can try out yourself.

# WHAT IS THE KAMA SUTRA?

The original Kama Sutra text is not just a smutty guide to sex, but is actually quite an in-depth text about society and ethics. Kama is a word meaning sexual love and it is only one of three elements that form the basic tenants of the Kama Sutra: the other two are: Artha-which is about the basics you need to survive (including food and housing) and Dharma-which simply means ethics. These elements were all seen as interrelated and necessary for a strong society. The Kama Sutra didn't just teach people about lovemaking, marriage and courtship but also the ethics of sex and how you should behave, including refraining from adultery and multiple partners.

Sexual love was seen as central because it's how we create families either literally or figuratively through marriage. For many of us, and it's safe to say all of the readers of this book, sex is an integral part of a relationship. Since sex is so fundamental to the building blocks of society it makes sense to get it right so to speak. The Kama Sutra understood the important of sex as a continual journey between two lovers whereby they grew closer, understood the other better and were continually exploring themselves via their partner. One of the problems with the Cosmo approach to Kama Sutra is that it looks only at the physical but it doesn't try to contextualize its significance. The positions of Kama Sutra are important because they teach us to explore and they usually require a deeper level of intimacy and trust. The positions are not the cause of this deepness though; they are just a conduit for your sexual awakening.

## Spirituality

What is important with the Kama Sutra is how it brings together the physical and spiritual elements of sex. This can be off putting to some people and is probably why the spiritual element is omitted from the flashy magazines, but it is not as mystical as it might sound. You already know that relationships and lovemaking are comprised of mental and spiritual components. There is no physical way in which a husband or wife is related. It's a symbolic and mental connection but it is also one that we see as the coupling of two identities or spirits. There is something about a romantic relationship that is inherently spiritual. We see this during lovemaking as well. When you have sex you are not just having sex with a lump of warm, blood-filled flesh. There is also a person there who you know on an entirely mental level, and that is also who you are making love to and is what makes sex so much more intense than solo lovemaking.

In Kama Sutra you are trying to be more attune to the spiritual element of lovemaking, so you are more present to what is happening and so that you enjoy it more. We might come to Kama Sutra hoping for a better way to get off, but this is almost the opposite of what Kama Sutra teaches. You should come to orgasm through lovemaking not because it was the destination (and you found a very sensitive sex position that makes your reach it quicker), but because there was nothing else your body could do at the point that you reach orgasm. When you try a new position you shouldn't just be focused on how you couple up below, but also how you now approach your partner differently and the way the body feels differently to you now.

## A new approach to sex

You should begin to re-examine sex, beginning with what sex is. If sex for you is just penetration, then you will not get very much out of Kama Sutra. You should see sex, instead, as a prolonged ritual that begins with light touching on the couch and continues into the later hours where you are collapsed together and just barely moving. The ritual of sex is important in the Kama Sutra and it is something you need to prepare for, but also not allow it to become predictable by focusing on the sheer mechanical nature of your body during sex. One of the most interesting aspects about tantric sex or Kama Sutra is just how un-kinky it is. It has very few elements of submission or control, it requires connection and light kissing and attention to cuddling. The positions are designed so that you both get as much pleasure as possible while continually filling each other with your shared love. You will not find yourself enjoying degrading a partner here because many of the positions require you to both make yourself vulnerable or to take control.

One of the reasons that Kama Sutra is so good for many relationships is because you can only take it slow and you have to relax to be able to carry out many of the positions. Without complete arousal you cannot deeply penetrate a partner in the ways a lot of the positions require. It would just be too painful because the female body in particular needs to expand in size as arousal increases. This is where the sex and the spirituality come together and it is how it improves your sex life. You are forced to be fully primed for sexual activity to carry out the Kama Sutra and it makes you take things slower and makes you confront parts of the body in a loving

10

and non-aggressive way. A lot of Kama Sutra positions will bring you face to face with the behind, quite literally, but you will approach it in a way that asks you to be gentle and to approach these parts as areas that you can both enjoy. Kama Sutra asks you to take the time to enjoy your partner and to get pleasure from their pleasure, and to also treat sex as an adventure that keeps on going.

# PRACTICING KAMA SUTRA

The Kama Sutra in its entirety is far more complex than the previous chapter suggests and is in truth a religious text; some people also couple it with teachings about Chakras and other eastern practices. In some senses though, it is no more complex than trying to have sex that is more sensual and considerate so that the power of your lovemaking spreads out into your relationship. The theory is interesting and enlightening but as with so many things practice is just as important, if not better. By trying out positions you will start to feel more connected to your partner and more comfortable around them without having to understand why it is happening. It is important though, that you practice Kama Sutra properly and not just as a checklist of things to try. This chapter will give you some simple guidance in your approach to the positions, so you get the most out of them.

## 10 Days of Lovemaking

During a couple's honeymoon, the Kama Sutra recommends that people take 10 days to get to know their partner with each day focusing on a different part of the body, beginning with caressing on the first day, heavier petting the second, kissing on the third and working your way up towards sex and exploration. This isn't necessary for everyone but it does show the principle that is behind Kama Sutra and what we need to do when following in its footsteps. We need to be able to understand why the positions we are trying are so pleasurable and also how to use them to their full advantages. Simply positioning yourself in a certain way will not dramatically increase your sex life but being aware of your partner and yourself will.

**Arousal**

As mentioned above full arousal is important to using the positions properly, not just because this will give you greater enjoyment but it will also be necessary to carry out some of the positions pain free. The cervix can be touched with a lot of these positions if you engage them too quickly; which can be painful. However, arousal is not just something that needs to be focused on for the female's sake, but also the males. We can sometimes be led into thinking that if we can do something then we are doing it right. There is no real definition of what sex is, so you most likely can't do it wrong, but you can more-or-less have sex without achieving full arousal. Women are usually all too aware of this, but men should be as well because they are able to have intercourse without being fully erect and often settle for a quick and easy goal, when something slower would be more satisfying.

The male's sexual response is actually more similar to the female's than is often thought. Relaxation, foreplay and intimacy will also increase his enjoyment of sex. Kama Sutra teaches that lovemaking should never be rushed and there is good reason for thinking this, but it is perhaps a bit too far. There are many types of lovemaking and we are capable of compartmentalizing ourselves so that we can enjoy a so-called quickie as much as a three hour long ritualistic lovemaking session complete with massage oils and soft pipe music. In fact, one thing the Kama Sutra does not teach that is good to keep in mind is that sex should not always be an attempt to reach the spiritual highs of tantric sex, because that can be too much pressure – you are allowed to have no-frills sex without worrying that you don't love your partner enough. You should, nevertheless, put out the fancy silverware when you are trying to use advanced sex positions.

## Breathing

There are lots of things to consider when you are trying to intensify arousal and foreplay. Something that is often ignored in Western cultures is breathing, which is relegated to the boring scientific role of keeping us alive. In Eastern cultures we bring rejuvenation with each breath and it is considered a bridge between spiritual and physical. Taking control of your breathing is important for a lot of reasons during sex. It allows you to slow down and focus, this can be especially important for men that are trying to delay orgasm. It is also a good idea to be aware of your partner's breathing. Sex is usually best when it is done in synch. You should try to maintain a similar breathing pattern if possible. A good technique is to lie together and try to match each other's breathing and to bring yourself back to this point every so often during lovemaking.

## Sensuality

All of our senses are important during lovemaking but this is often ignored. Touch is the most obvious and even this is sometimes under used. Many people are uncomfortable with their bodies – if you are the kind of person that must wear a t-shirt during sex or feels they need to have the lights off, then you might need to address this kind of thing first before you try to turn to fancy sex positions. Even people that are more outwardly comfortable with their bodies are self-conscious about a lot of it. You should take the time to explore your partner's body and have them explore yours – touching, tasting and even smelling every part. Communication is also important here. You should be able to tell a partner what you don't like about yourself so they can assure you that they like it (and they will). Kama Sutra can be very useful in increasing communication between couples because it breaks down certain barriers, and you then have an openness that is naturally carried over to less erotic matters.

It is also important to use the other sense at your disposal; you can practice with this by playing with sensory deprivation. Perhaps taking turns being blindfolded or avoiding the use of your hands whenever possible, so that you get a new appreciation for parts of the body we ignore. The bouquets of sex are also fascinating if you stop being afraid of them, and you should try to savor the rich tapestry of scents that your partner has.

**Coreplay**

Oral sex is something that is not always explicitly explored in the positions. It definitely is in some of them, but it is also something they can't properly express with still images. Understanding what makes your partner purr will enhance your lovemaking dramatically, and taking the time to ensure you are both enjoying yourselves is integral. Many people recommend performing oral sex before any real intercourse begins, and using it as a gap between foreplay and intercourse that gives a heightened awareness of each other. Many couples don't communicate properly during this, which is odd because it's so central to enjoying what is going on. Oral sex is at the heart of making their pleasure your pleasure.

## Planning

Planning sex can seem a little odd at first, after all, wasn't part of the idea to get rid of predictability? It is true that you want to get rid of predictability, but that is predictable sex that will leave you predictably unsatisfied and distant. When properly employing Kama Sutra techniques you will need privacy, forethought and time, which is something you are not going to get with a spontaneous quickie most of the time. Using Kama Sutra positions and paying attention to your body and your partner's needs are all part of creating a ritual, and deciding on a time and place when you will have sex for a very long time, not only enhances this, but creates a sense of anticipation and excitement that makes sex more enjoyable and allows you to expand on things you have tried in the past.

# THE 40 POSITIONS

Below are 40 Kama Sutra positions for you to try out with your partner. How you wish to engage in them is up to you, and whether you want to change them up is your preference. It is best to rotate through positions, keeping in mind where the most sensation and pleasure is being received as well as who takes most of the strain or does the heavy lifting. The effort required does vary and it is often best to start with the more mutual and simple positions and move into a more strenuous one later. Also, contrary to what a lot of films or pornography might suggest, there is no need to have non-stop penetration until orgasm once you have reached that stage. It is perfectly enjoyable to pause and revert back to coreplay or foreplay, or even to just caress for a while. The most important thing is that you do what feel right for you.

# 1. THE KNEE-ROCK

This is called the knee-rock because of the action it makes the man perform. The woman lies on her back and brings her knees up to her chest, she can cross them if she likes. Almost like the fetal position but don't think about that. The man then kneels in front of her and rests against the back of her thighs while he thrusts. With this position the woman receives full contact from the man and gets maximum sensation on her vulva, clitoris and thigh. This should not be used for too long as the woman will not be able to move too much and it is also quite an intense position. It also leads to quite deep penetration which some women will not enjoy.

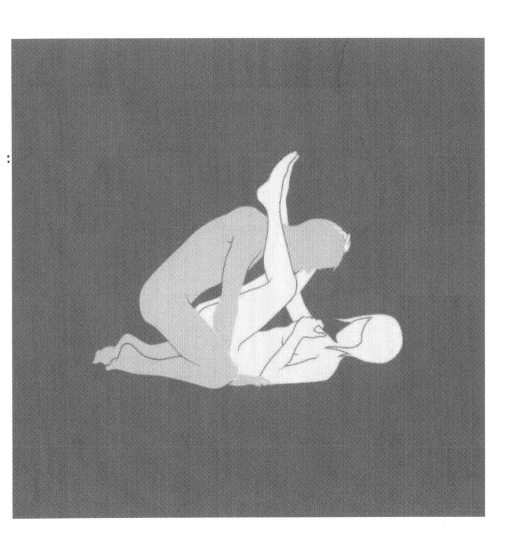

## 2. THE TURTLE

The lovers sit face-to-face, almost like they are at a prayer meeting. Then, as carefully as possible, they place their feet up to each other's chest and hold hands. While in this position they are able to make love while gently rocking back and forth. It is a position that both will enjoy but it can require some practice and could result in you falling over. Be carefulle with the position of your legs and hands as you don't want to accidentally kick or hurt the other person. It is a position that requires subtlety and gentleness. It is called the turtle because of the strange hump it will make with your bodies.

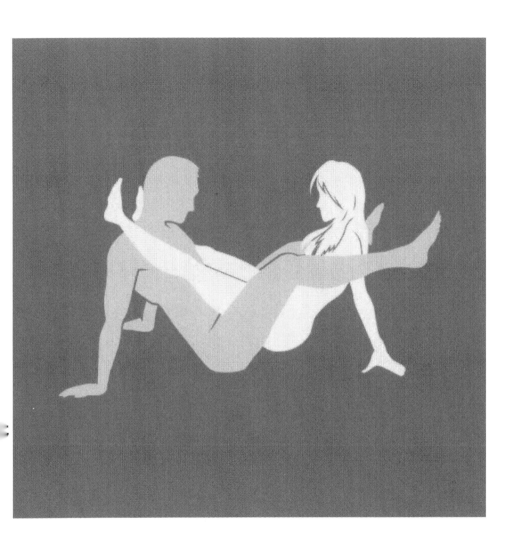

# 3. THE PARALLEL

The two lovers lie on their sides face-to-face with their legs straight. They attempt to touch at every point possible from their knees to their face. The lovers then join together while maintaining the side-to-side pose and proceed to make love with gentle movements and thrusting. It is good to try and use your hands for just caressing rather than creating movement so that you can enjoy the tenderness of this position. You can experiment with your bodies by moving and squeezing your thighs and hips together, as well as enjoying the sensation of moving your genitals into different positions, which can better stimulate the clitoris or even try to tease it.

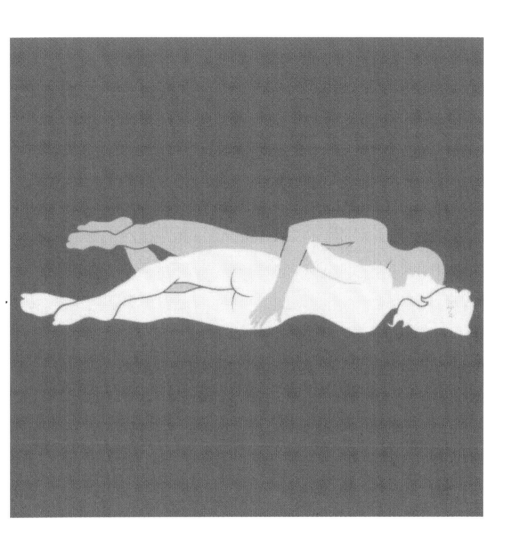

# 4. THE DOG

You're probably familiar with this one. Its less sophisticated cousin is known as 'doggy style'. That might seem crude but it is actually quite close to the Kama Sutra's intention which is to look to the animals of nature for inspiration. Quite simply the woman gets more or less on her hands and knees, and the man takes her from behind. Both lovers are able to alter their position as they please, perhaps the man lowering himself further down so they are touching closer. This position is fun and energetic but it should also be used in conjunction with other positions that allow more face-to-face intimacy.

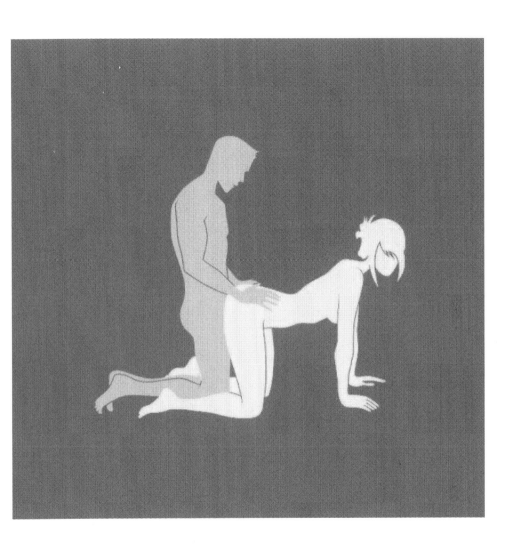

## 5. THE THIGH PRESS

This position is similar to the first one but different enough to be considered an entirely new one. The man sits on the floor with his legs stretched out in front of him in a v-shape. The woman lowers herself onto him and sits between his thighs. The man then takes her thighs and holds them together and maneuvers them together for further lovemaking. This position uses a lot of face contact and brings you very close together, but it also restricts movement and may create deep penetration. It also opens itself up to a lot of caressing and can require quite a lot of physical activity to get the most out of it.

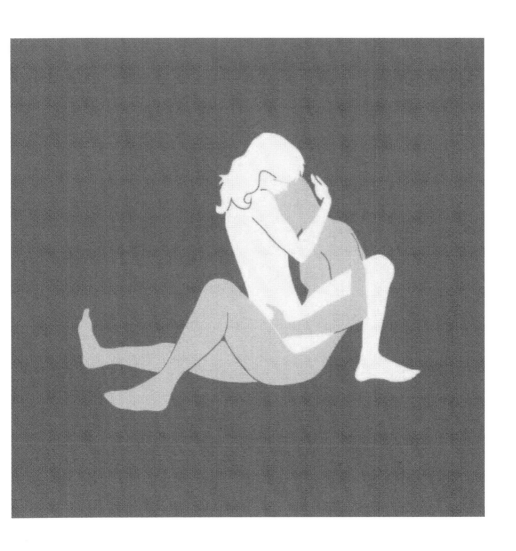

## 6. THE HOLLYWOOD

This position can be an exhausting one and might need to come with an age warning. The man holds the woman up against a wall and she embraces him so they can make love. It's called the Hollywood because it is a favorite of films because of its energy and novelty – and because it can be a bit impractical. With significant height difference this can require a lot of strength and the man may be supporting the woman's weight quite a lot. She will be required to hold onto him properly and distribute her weight evenly. This position is recommended as a beginning one that will then fall into something more sustainable.

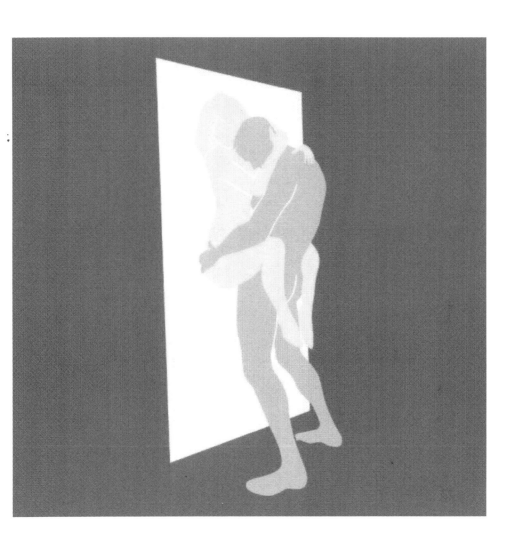

# 7. THE LONGBOW

This position is so-named because of the angle that it puts the woman's body in. She places a pillow under her head and pelvis so that she is curved. She then raises her legs and spreads them apart for him to enter. This is a fairly comfortable position that is not too dissimilar from a relatively conventional missionary position, but it enhances the pleasure of sex by using the pillow to direct the hips so that the g-spot and clitoris are stimulated well by the man. It can be useful to keep pillows around for use in other types of lovemaking, especially oral sex.

## 8. THE CHALK OUTLINE

In this position the lovers lie out in a star shape and then proceed to lie on top of each other, creating a satisfying sandwich effect. The name comes from the similarity to cartoon crime procedurals where a sprawled out body is chalked out for detectives. This is a very intense position and you have to be careful not to trap flesh under limbs, and that your weight is being distributed evenly. You will not be able to move too much but that will only encourage you to place attention on what you can move. This is quite a novel position but it is fun to play around with.

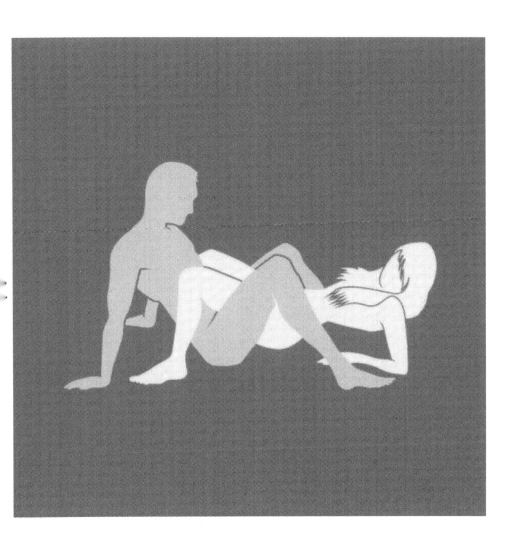

## 9. THE LOTUS

This is an important position and one you will hear often. It is often used as the foundation for another position and you will have likely tried it already, given a basic curiosity of what your body can do during lovemaking. The man sits more or less cross-legged and the woman sits on his lap and wraps her legs around him. Once you have connected together not much movement is required at all, and too much might even cause discomfort. A slow and gentle movement is all that is required. It is a position that encourages kissing of the face and other types of close intimacy. It is named because you supposedly look like the petals of a lotus – although it's not clear you will actually hold that kind of elegance when you try it.

## 10. THE RAISED LEG

This is a kind of variation on the lotus or a move that can be incorporated into it. Once again the man sits cross-legged and the woman sits in his lap, but instead of wrapping her legs around him she instead uses a hand to guide her leg back and forth. Be sure to use whichever side you find is dominant, or easy for you and start this by taking it slowly. It is an interesting position because it allows stimulation without the usual kind of control over what you are doing, so it feels more natural in a way. It can look a little bizarre but it is definitely a position to try out if you are looking for new experiences. It might not allow for the same kind of caressing.

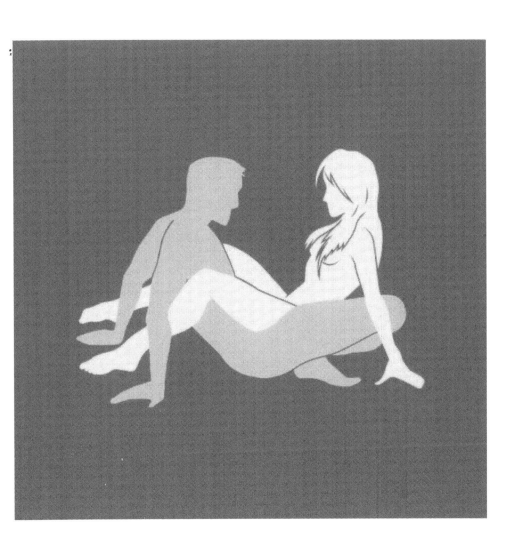

## 11. THE SKYDIVE

Sometimes Kama Sutra positions are beautiful and gentle and elegant. However, sometimes they have you lying down and pulling your ankles from behind you. This is what the woman does here; it can be useful to have a pillow involved here. The woman will have to try and grasp her ankles from behind and the man enters her from behind. It puts both of you in a strange curvature that creates a different sensation. This is called the Skydive because the woman will have her limbs backwards like she is in mid-fall, and the man will look like he is trying to have sex with someone that is currently mid-fall. This position demands quite a bit of limberness on the woman's part.

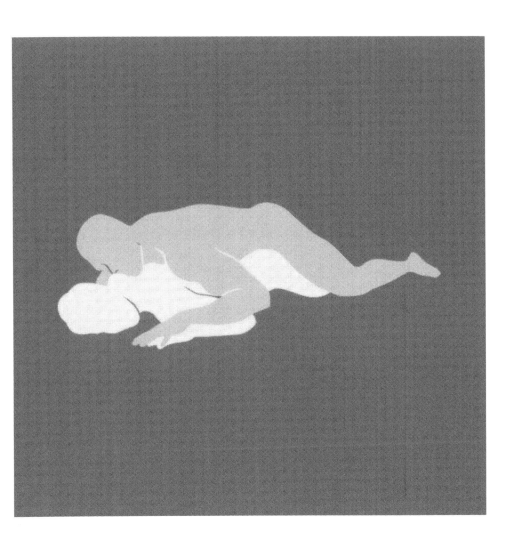

## 12. THE HOLY X

This position is named after the fact that two 'V's when stuck together at their tip make an 'X'. In this position the man sits with his legs in front like a V and the woman lowers onto him and extends her legs out behind him so that they are also like a V. The man may then lower her slightly back and rock her slightly, or she might like to lean forward and gently rock herself. Because you are essentially sat on each other like a pair of Barbie dolls, movements of your lower half are extremely restricted but there can be a lot of pleasure in this position. It allows for both of you to have a very gentle lovemaking, and for a lot of eye-contact and intimacy.

## 13. THE SWAN

Although the Kama Sutra told us to copy animals it turns out that many animals stick to a fairly familiar doggy style, and they aren't too big on experimentation. So we've taken to naming our positions after the vague animal shape they represent. The swan does this perfectly. You do this position by having the man lay on the ground, perhaps with a pillow under his lower back or neck. The woman then sits on him so that they connect. However, she does this so that both her legs are to one side of him and her arms work him like a weight. She then has to slide up and down on him, but not in the same way that you might in a cowgirl. The two lovers will then resemble a swan lightly bobbing on a lake.

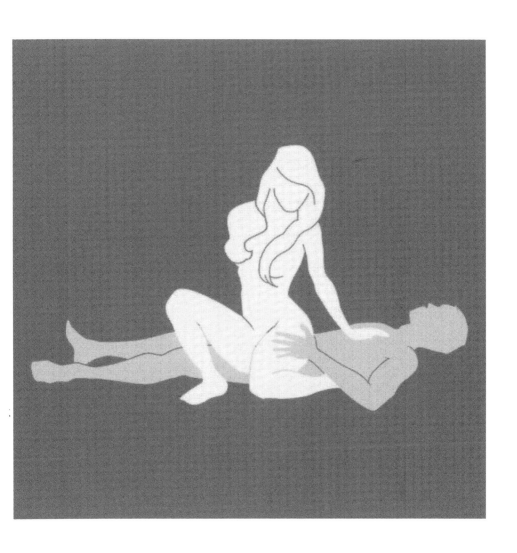

## 14. THE BEE

For this position the man lies down facing upwards and the woman crouches over him with her knees up and her feet on his body. She lowers herself onto him using her arms to support her by holding on to his thigh or knee area. In this position she is able to move in several directions and give lots of pleasure to the man, but also direct him so that she is getting as stimulated as possible. This position requires a bit of self discipline so that the woman remembers to try and pleasure them both, and maintains the position for a while instead of giving in to something more like the conventional cowgirl.

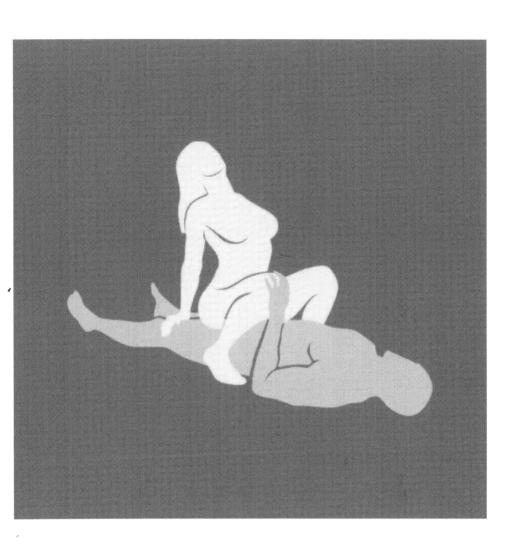

## 15. THE BULL

Named after the way one of the lover's arms will be spread into a beautiful horn shape. With this position the man sits on the floor with his legs in front of him. He might even like to begin by reclining a little. The woman will then lower herself on to him with her legs stretched out as if to do the splits, and leaning forward to touch his toes. This will take quite some adjustment depending on the lover's height and flexibility. It is a position to take slowly to make sure that nobody feels too much discomfort too quickly, but it can increase intensity in a way that similar, but less involved, positions don't.

## 16. THE YODA

This is a fun position that will result in quite a lot of friction, so be prepared. The man lies down straight on his back and then the woman sits on top of him in that special way but with her legs crossed. She then uses his thighs for leverage and oscillates up and down while maintaining the cross-legged stance. Called the Yoda because the woman adopts an almost Jedi pose while appearing to levitate up and down. This is one of the less practical positions, but it is a fun one to try out and might be good as part of an exercise regimen.

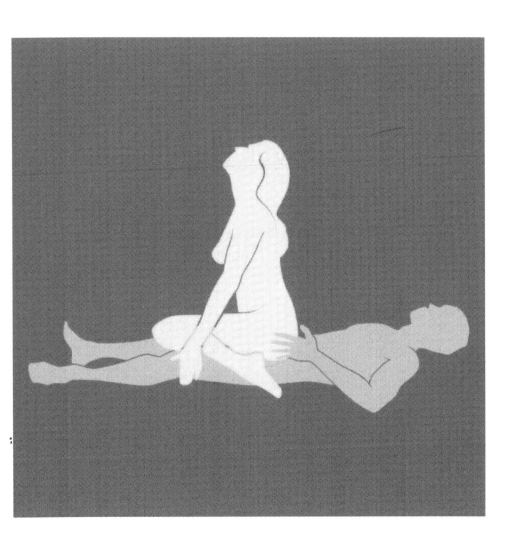

49

## 17. THE STATUE

This is similar to the Hollywood in that both partners will be stood up and against a wall, but it has quite a different mechanic behind it. Instead of the man hoisting the woman up for smoother thrusting, the woman will instead spread her legs apart while standing and lightly clinging to his shoulders. The height factor is important here, but it works well as a compromise to those that found the Hollywood too strenuous. It's a good position for foreplay, especially if you are starting outside of the bedroom. It's probably not too suitable for the entirety of your lovemaking, but it is good as a transitional position.

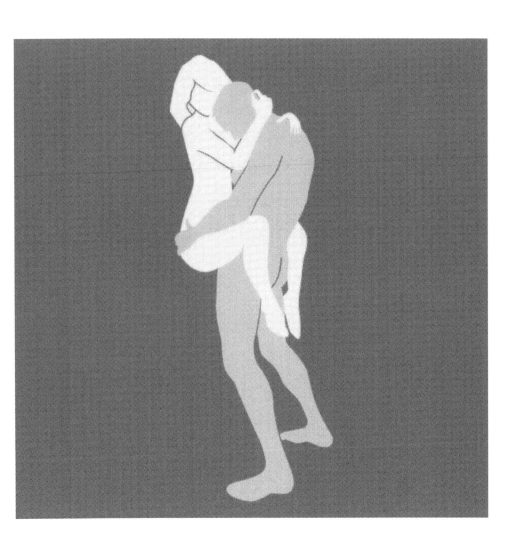

# 18. CROUCHING TIGER

This position is a work of art if done properly but requires serious coordination. The man sits with his knees apart but his feet nearly touching, like he is sat watching a river flow past. The woman comes between his knees and faces him while squatting, so that her feet are touching him at his buttocks. The lovers will then need to hold each other: the man by holding her feet and the woman by reaching back to grab the man's feet. To get proper thrusting during this position will require quite a lot of movement and energy, but it is a very exciting position that brings you closer together.

## 19. THE PISTON

This is another position that puts a lot of effort in the woman's court, especially if the man is happy to sit back and relax. Which is where the position begins. The man sits down and leans back like he is on a recliner and supporting himself with his arms. The woman then sits on top of him with her feet on either side. She then uses her legs like steel springs to go up and down, using her arms where she sees fit as support.

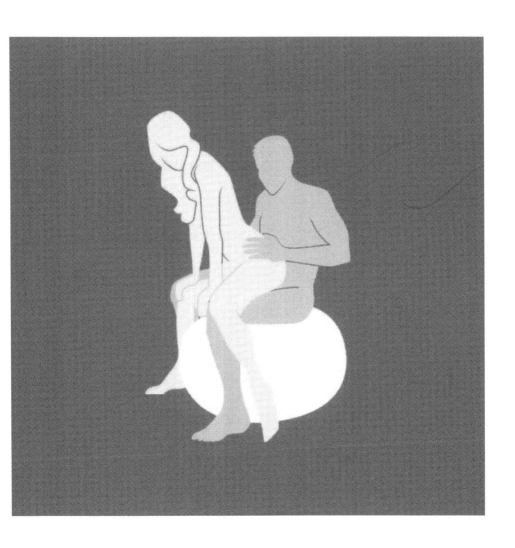

## 20. THE DOUBLE ELBOW

This one can sound like a mess but works surprisingly well in practice. The man begins by sitting with his legs spread apart but not so far that the woman cannot sit in his lap. The woman sits in his lap while his legs are still in a sitting position. She raises her legs to around where his elbows naturally rest, and then wraps her legs around his back. The man then needs to support her legs, back, and neck. To get the most from this position the man will need to rock back and forth rather than thrust.

## 21. THE WHEEL

This position is bizarre, fun, and magical. It might not be something you want to do for too long and it requires a lot of effort, but it needs to be tried at least once. It works well as a transitional position or to break things up. It is simple to describe but harder to practice with grace. The man lies down like a starfish and the woman sits on top. The woman then uses her arms and legs to spin herself around – not unlike a wheel.

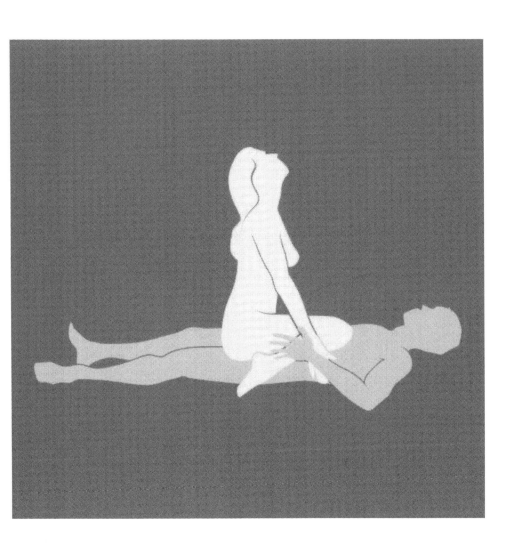

## 22. THE ALTAR

So far a lot of these positions have required a lot of effort from the woman but this one is, so to speak, all man. The man needs to kneel down with his legs in a slight V shape so that he is sat on his ankle, with care not to cut off circulation. The woman lowers herself into his lap until they are joined together while she uses her arms to support herself from behind. He then lifts her legs up at the knee and moves in whatever way the lovers find comfortable.

## 23. THE NO-HANDS TELEPHONE

For this position the man sits or kneels down so that the woman is able to have as much unobstructed access to him as possible. She then lies in front of him and places one leg on his corresponding shoulder, so that it rests next to his face like someone speaking on the telephone with no hands. Lovemaking then commences, and the man positions the woman accordingly and occasionally they might decide that she should switch shoulders which will take quite a bit of coordination. Depending on your commitment there are various options for how much effort is required on either behalf.

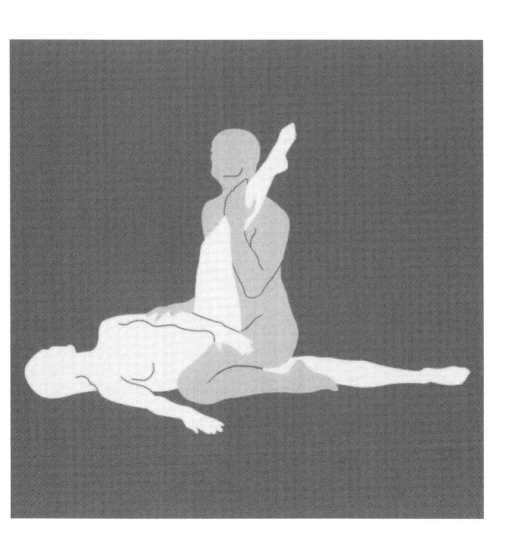

## 24. THE THREE LEGS OF LOVE

This is another standing position but with another variation that makes it more complex, and doesn't necessarily require a wall as a prop. The man and woman stand facing each other like they might want to dance. The woman raises her leg and rests it against his thigh and he takes her thigh with his hand so that he can keep her stable and move her body in and out of his. You may require a piece of furniture to steady yourselves but the adventurous lover will try this, at least once, free standing. An interesting but difficult position.

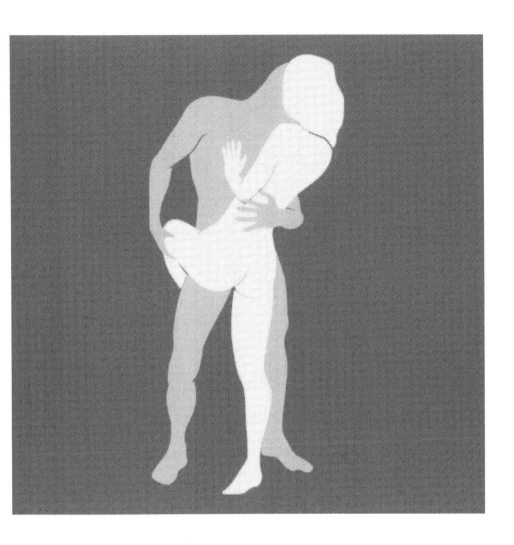

## 25. THE WHEELBARROW

You can probably imagine how this position goes down between the lovers. It is a bit like a wheelbarrow race, but with no plan on getting anywhere. How you want to ease in to this position is up to you, and your flexibility and upper-body strength. Essentially, the man must be near standing while the woman is facing away from him and her legs are at the height of his hips. This is somewhat like doggy style, but both of the lovers are raised higher than that position usually requires and could move forwards like an actual wheelbarrow if they wished.

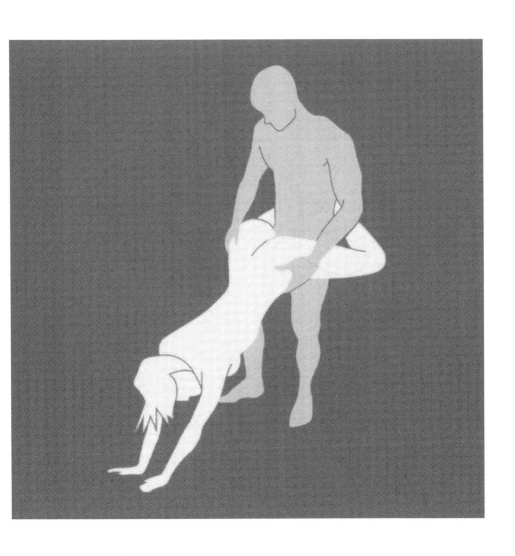

## 26. THE SAIL

This is a simple and very passionate position that could just as easily be called the 'clinging on for dear life' position. The man stands and the woman puts her arm around his neck like she wants to whisper a secret into his ear. She then lifts herself up and wraps her legs around his middle. He must hold her by the buttocks or thigh and hold her to him like a sail on a boat. This position could result in you capsizing if you are not slow to enter into it, and can take a lot of energy and balance – but try to avoid using furniture as support if you can for the full effect.

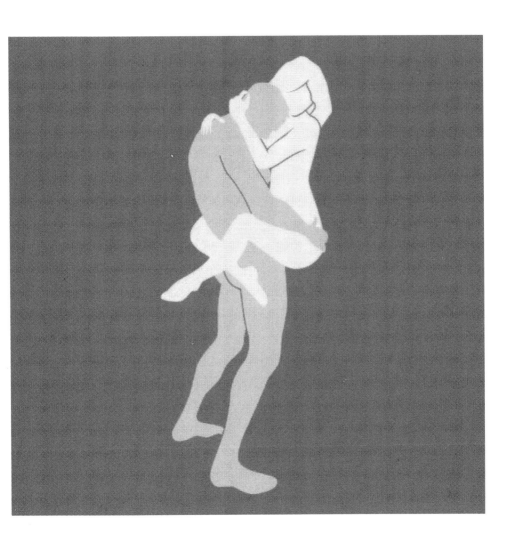

## 27. THE GIRAFFE

No position with this name is going to be easy. Like many positions the woman takes a striking elegant pose like a ballerina, and the man finds a way to work around this. In this instance, she punches one fist in the air like Superman and lifts the opposite leg as though she is hopping. The man comes to her from behind and holds the raised leg by her thigh and takes her other side from just below the armpit. This position allows for maneuverability while standing, but is still a standing position and so it is difficult to maintain for too long, especially for couch potato lovers.

## 28. THE COW

What is the difference between a dog and a cow when making love? It's the question that defines the existence of these two similar but crucially different positions. The answer is the cow must remain on all fours. For this position the woman stands on all fours in the front of the man who must be almost fully standing where he will proceed to take her from behind. From here you might like to move into doggy style which is perhaps easier, and takes less stability and strength to enjoy. It's useful to have lots of variations in your arsenal, however.

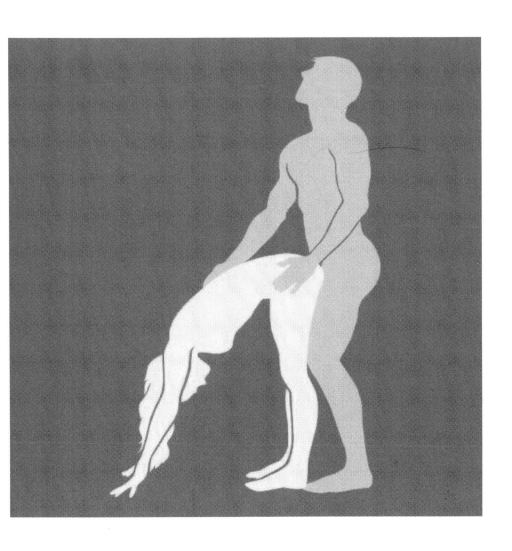

## 29. THE IMPOSSIBLE

This is a novel position that is easier said than done sometimes, and may not work if done without precision. This position is similar to what in lesbian circles is known as 'scissoring'. The lovers begin by lying down and taking the top and tail sleeping position, with their feet near each other's heads. You then need to lower yourself into each other. It is best if the woman is on her side and the man slides down more like a starfish. You will need to get over the problem of friction from the thighs here, but it can be done.

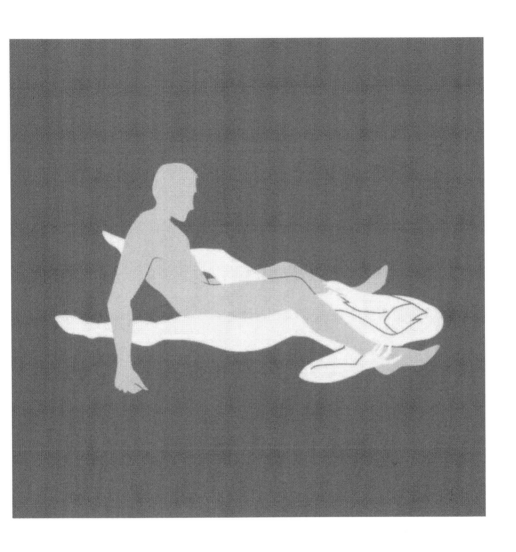

## 30. THE BENDED KNEE

Like most simple things the complexities are hidden. In this position the woman lies back in slight or complete recline and, for want of a more elegant phrase, spreads her legs with bent knees. The man then enters her with gentleness and intimacy, and tries not to cause any unnecessary discomfort. This is quite a natural position but it is one where care needs to be taken because it can be easy to penetrate too far, too quickly.

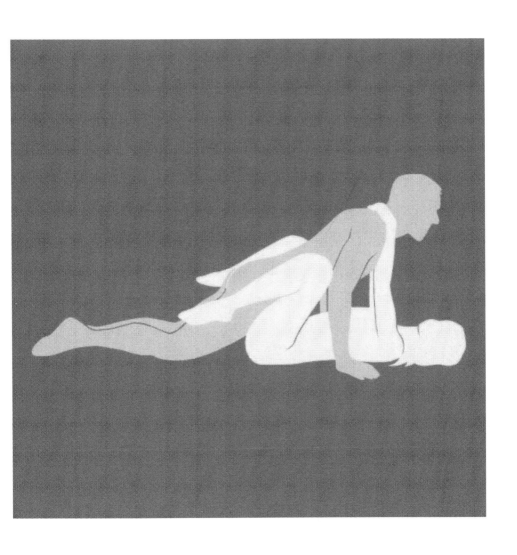

# 31. THE ELEPHANT

The elephant position belongs in the doggy style
family along with the cow and is possibly the
easiest of the three, and something many people
might assume after a prolonged use of the dog
position. The woman kneels in front of the man
with her legs bent and then stretches her arms
forward, and low to the ground almost like prayer
– like an elephant's trunk. The man takes her from
behind and has lots of maneuverability, and is
even able to embrace the woman quite tenderly.

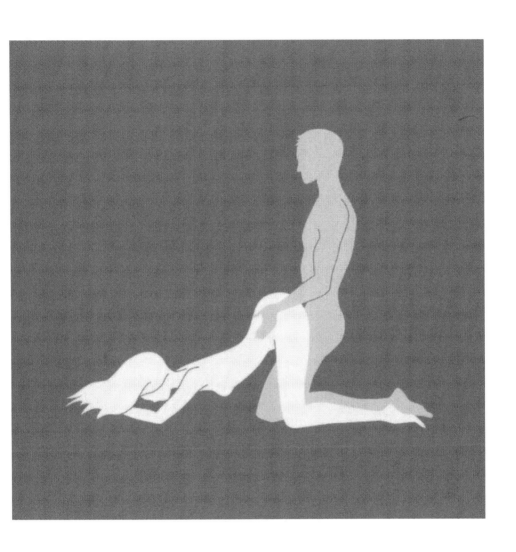

## 32. THE BALLERINA

This is a tricky position that really is not for everyone. It conventionally requires the woman to be limber, but it might be fun to reverse positions and see if you can both do it. The man lies down in a slight recline and the woman lowers herself on to him with one leg on the floor beside him and the other brought up to as near to her head as she can reach – like the kick in a dance of swan lake. She will need to steady the leg with her hand and this position will need to be taken slowly. The man should also be careful to support her and to not get carried away with the athleticism on display.

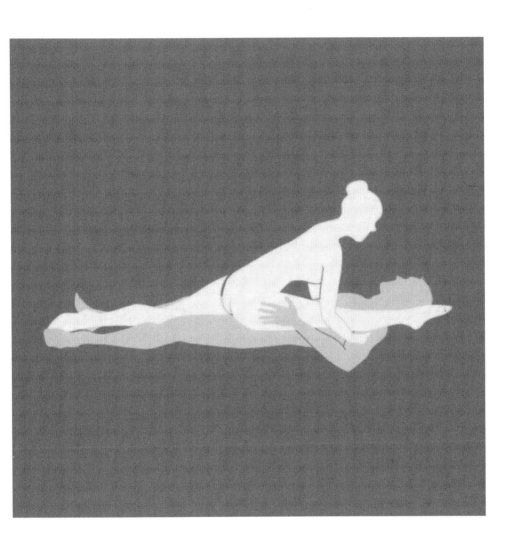

## 33. THE BICYCLE

This position is named after a lazy weekend bike ride around a park. Like so many of the positions, it begins with the man lying on the floor, helpless to the woman's advances. The woman lowers herself on, facing him and placing her legs on either side of him below his raised arms. She then leans back with both hands on the floor on either side of him. She needn't actually peddle him, but there are many ways to play in this position.

## 34. THE DIVERS

This can be a bit of an awkward position because it is about as full contact as you can get, but it is an interesting position to try out. To perform this one either the man or the woman can lay on the ground – often the man does because he is a better load-bearing creature. You then need to stretch out to your full length while facing each other and touch your hands together (and feet if your height allows this). In this position you will have to carefully make love, but it will be a very intimate type of lovemaking.

## 35. THE PRONE POSITION

This is a very comfy position that is sort of the logical conclusion of the doggy style family. The woman sits upright and then lowers herself on to the man, so that she forms a v shape around him and fits onto him snuggly. She should then be able to grip his feet and he is able to thrust and control her hips. As with a lot of these positions, it does run the risk of losing some intimacy which is never the point of Kama Sutra.

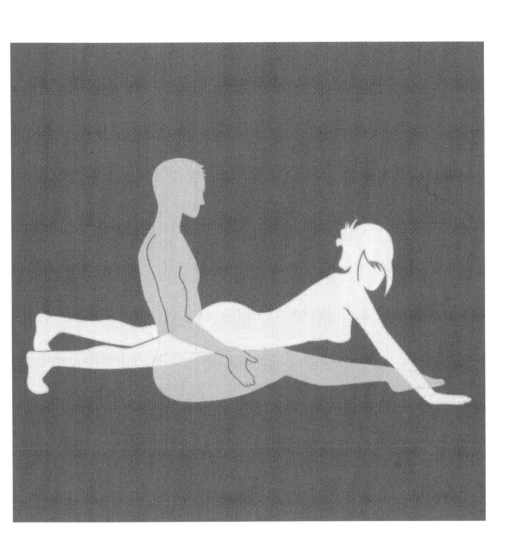

## 36. THE MIRROR

There is something oddly juvenile about this position, but nothing particularly juvenile about its enactment. The man and the woman lie down so their heads are at opposite sides and their buttocks are practically touching. The lovers then form arches with their legs so their feet are touching at the sole and they are holding their legs up with their knees. Being inside each other is not always easy with this position, but that does not always have to be the main aim of sex. You can try other things while in this position or enjoy the foot wrestle that will ensue.

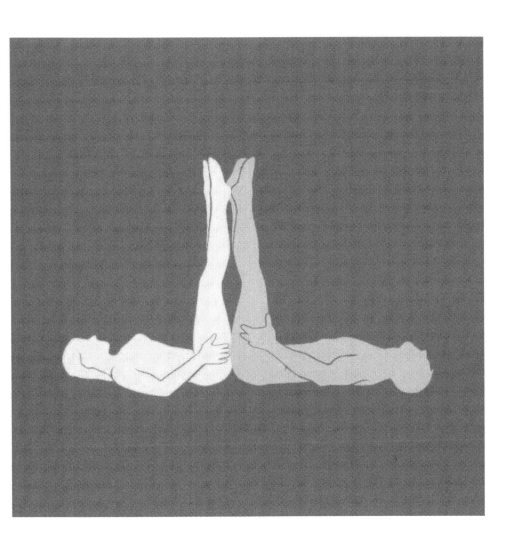

# 37. THE ROCK STAR

This is a good position because it allows a lot of intimacy while also allowing a lot of freedom, and stimulation of the vulva. The woman sits on her heels and lays back with her arms out so that she looks like she is performing a rock star slide with a guitar on stage. The man is then free to engage her and become very close to her body and face. Don't keep at this one too long, as she might start to lose circulation in her legs if you are not careful. You could do this position in reverse if you liked.

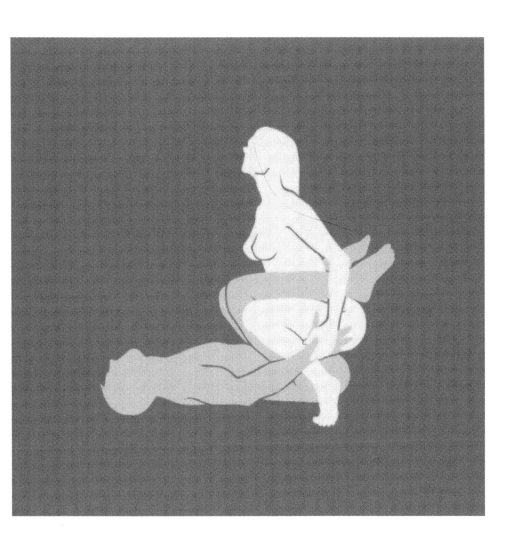

## 38. THE PULL BAR

This is a position that is great if you want a real workout and you are both quite strong. The man sets up to do a position similar to the missionary, but he is on all fours and raised up from the surface you are lying on. The woman will be lying underneath him and will have to raise her pelvis up to meet his, and pull herself up on his back. Be careful to pull yourself up to him and to not just pull him down towards the ground.

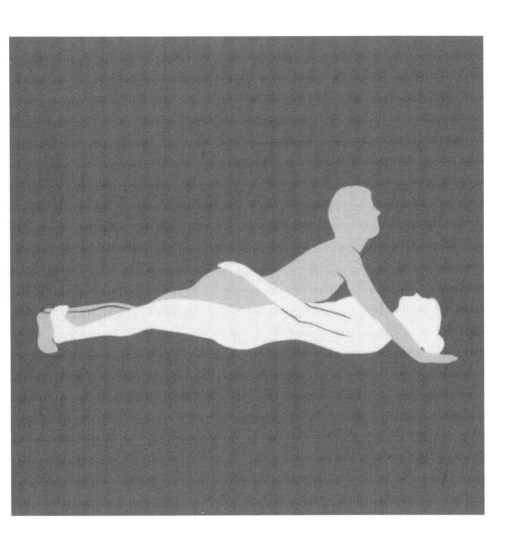

# 39. THE PILLOW FORT

This is a nice and extremely cozy position, good for winter nights when you are trying to stay warm. It's essentially the dog position but with a twist. You stack a series of pillows high enough so that the woman can bend over them and enjoy their natural spring. The man comes behind and has his legs on the outside. This is a soft and springy position that can be very relaxing to perform.

## 40. THE LEG INSPECTOR

This is a position that allows for almost maximum penetration while also giving your legs a good stretch. It's quite simple to achieve, but you will need a special apparatus. To do this position the woman will have to lie on a table or high bed, or another hip high piece of furniture. She will want to have her buttocks at the edge of the table. She will then place her legs together and place them high in the air as though she is sitting. He will then approach and join together with her. Since her legs are pressed together it will amplify the sensation of being together and he can use her legs as a kind of support.

# CONCLUSION

You should now have a good understanding of what the Kama Sutra is, and what it can do for your sex life. It is a practical mantra for you to come back to often but it is also a spiritual one that, if you allow it, can really amplify the feelings you have for your lover. Remember that when trying out the positions, you should always take your time and make sure you are both comfortable when trying something new. Kama Sutra is about being closer together and being more present during lovemaking. By focusing too much on the novelty of the positions you can end up distancing yourself more. Think of it like building a house with your partner. It is, of course, nice to have a kitchen full of utensils and extra rooms but you need to use that space to have a life together. It's not good if you decide to live in separate rooms. The Kama Sutra positions are like this. It's no good exploring each other and trying new positions if you use it to start having these separate sexual experiences where you are both concerned about getting a position right.

Kama Sutra, more than anything else, should be fun. Sometimes the fun can get lost if there is too much effort or too much pressure to enjoy sex, or to have fantastic sex with pelvis-shattering orgasms. If you find you are not enjoying something, then stop. Not every position will work for every person, and they are not made as a one size fits all strategy. If you find you are uncomfortable for psychological reasons, be open with your partner.

Most of all, remember to love each other and to become closer in your lovemaking.

Made in the USA
Las Vegas, NV
25 November 2022

60252768R00057